First Lady

A Workbook and Journal

First Lady

A Workbook and Journal

Rochelle Pearson

Copyright

Printed in the United States of America

First Printing, 2018

ISBN-13: 978-1-947656-60-4

ISBN10: 1947656600

The Butterfly Typeface Publishing
PO BOX 56193
Little Rock Arkansas 72215
www.butterflytypeface.com
butterflytypeface.imw@gmail.com

Dedication

To God be the glory for all that He has done in my life; for implanting the gift of writing in my belly and for allowing me now to give birth to that gift. To the strong women who taught me that the truth will set you free. To my children who have made me the woman that I am today. To my beloved daughter, Sharifa Asha, who graced us for only such a short time, but while here on earth with us showed what strength, perseverance and fearless meant - sleep in Peace, until we meet again. To my grandmother who introduced me to church at an early age; she saw in me what I didn't see in myself. Thank you for allowing me to be me; Mrs. Bertha Lee Robinson Pearson, your prayers over me did not go in vain.

"for you created my inmost being; you knit me together in my mother's womb. I praise you because I am fearfully and wonderfully made; your works are wonderful, I know that full well."

Psalm 139:13-14

Table of Contents

Foreword

I believe I was 'destined' to publish this book.

Long before I knew of Rochelle Pearson, I was introduced to a First Lady. We became great friends and she trusted me with information and feelings that she hadn't previously shared. Later she and I took a journey together where I found myself in the midst of a "First Lady" convention. As I sat there thinking, "I don't belong here. I'm not a First Lady," I got this overwhelming sense of a belonging. I realized I did belong and I was indeed a First Lady even though I wasn't married to a pastor.

What I've learned is that being a First Lady is a calling, a mindset, an obligation; not to the pastor or even to the congregation, but to God. A First Lady must be a servant to God, to her husband (if she's married), and not the least of which, to the people she has been called to inspire, encourage, and feed spiritually.

So you see, by the time I met Rochelle Pearson, I was prepared to publish this book.

This book is entertaining. It is shocking. But more than that, it will leave you with a sense of knowing and understanding. When you walk away from this book (and into the journal), I hope that you will have found what I found – a sense of purpose.

I believe it is the job of each of us to put away the stones we would throw and instead throw an empathetic arm around our sister when she is hurting and in need of an Earthly Angel.

Behind every big hat, flashy smile and gloved hand beats the heart of a woman just like you and me. This woman, though called to lead, serve and shepherd, sometimes needs to be able to be vulnerable. She needs a soft place to land. She needs to be heard and sometimes she may even need to cry.

If that woman is you, allow yourself to be loved. If that woman is someone you know – love her unconditionally.

Thank you, Rochelle Pearson, for allowing me to assist with your work and for shedding light in a place where darkness threatens to abide.

Oris M. Williams

Author/Publisher

Acknowledgment

To the First Lady,

Rest your hat and gloves; make yourself at home ...

R. Pearson

Introduction

In my book, First Lady, three women whose desire to be First Lady proved that all that glittered was not gold as once told.

Realization from the attention, the glamour, and the fame that accompanies being a First Lady came to a head. Each woman soon realized that being a First Lady was not all it was cracked up to be. The lies, deceit, the hurt, and the pain that come with being a First Lady forced them to face reality.

The defeats and triumphs of their story will highlight things in your life and help you to see your true self.

At the end of the day, one has to be true to self. Be you, live you, and do you in the truth and the spirit of life.

This workbook/journal is offered to you to assist you in your journey towards discovery of the real you. To be true to self, be you, live you and do you in truth and the spirit of life.

Rochelle Pearson

Here is where your

Journal

begins …

Your Thoughts

What does it really mean to be a First Lady? Is being married to a pastor the only way to be a First Lady? Elaborate on your response.

The First Lady Assignment

Were you trained to be a First Lady or were you born to be one? Explain your
answer.

The First Lady Assignment

Thoughts

Why do you think being a First Lady is such a coveted role?

Perfection

Do you feel the need to be perfect? Why or why not?

Marriages

Do you feel it is more difficult to be married to a Pastor? Why or why not?

Identification

Can you identify with any of the women in the *First Lady* story? How?

Children

Should you talk to children about what is going on in your marriage? Why or why not?

Children

Lies

What role do lies play in our lives? Have you told lies? What prompted you to tell them and how did it ultimately affect the situation?

Rochelle Pearson | 101

Sin

Is it necessary to confess your sins to others? Why or why not?

Truth

Is it harder to tell the truth to those you love?

Truth

Blame

In the story, *First Lady*, who was to blame regarding the marital issues in your opinion?

First Lady

Women vs Men

Do you think men have a harder time in marriage than women? Why or why not? And how so?

Changes

What needs to change regarding *First Ladies* in your opinion?

About the Author

A native of Brooklyn, New York, Rochelle Pearson spent her time divided between New York and South Carolina. Preaching the gospel has been a lifelong calling for Rochelle. She preached her trial sermon at the age of 12 for the African Methodist Episcopal Zion Denomination in South Carolina. (United in Fort Mill).

Soon after that her grandmother passed away in South Carolina, Rochelle returned to New York as a pre-teen, got caught up in a life where church was just a thought and survival became real. She became a teen mom, a young wife, and soon reality set in. A divorce and the responsibility of raising a child strengthened her to achieve what she has accomplished.

Pearson is familiar with lies, betrayals, abuse, and what it means to struggle to get what you want. However, she knew deep down that a better day was going to come.

She also knew that the truth does set you free.

Rochelle discovered her true self when she lost one of her daughters to cancer at the age of eight. After that death, a renewal, an awakening began. Rochelle returned to South Carolina and returned to the ministry where she has been ever since.

Rochelle strongly believes that your test and trials make way for your testimony. They give you a ministry to help others to overcome their struggles.

"My ministry," she boldly proclaims "is about leading others to the true and living God and teaching that we can have an abundant life here on earth. My mission is to empower and motivate men and women to tap into their true self. Once a person knows their truth, then they can live to their full potential."

Pearson holds degrees from the following: Borough of Manhattan Community College (New York, NY), ECPI College of Technology (Charlotte, NC), and Livingstone College (Salisbury, NC).

She currently lives in Key West, FL and serves as the Pastor of Cornish Memorial AME Zion Church and the Presiding Elder of the Key West District, where a variety of ministries are offered for all generations.

To contact Rochelle Pearson

Email: pearsonproductions1@gmail.com

Facebook: @PearsonProductions1

Word Angels Books

Is an imprint of

The Butterfly Typeface Publishing.

Contact us for all your

publishing & writing needs!

Iris M Williams

PO Box 56193

Little Rock AR 72215

www.butterflytypeface.com

50117542R00102

Made in the USA
Columbia, SC
01 February 2019